1. **Introduction**
   - Importance of a Website
   - Necessity of Building a Website

2. **Planning and Strategy**
   - Defining Goals and Objectives
   - Analyzing Target Audience

3. **Domain and Hosting**
   - Choosing a Domain Name
   - Types of Web Hosting

4. **Website Design**
   - Principles of User-Friendly Design
   - Importance of Responsive Design

5. **Content Creation**
   - Creating High-Quality Content
   - SEO-Friendly Content

6. **Development Tools and Platforms**
   - Website Builders vs. Custom Development
   - Choosing a CMS (Content Management System)

7. **Website Functionality**
   - Essential Features and Plugins
   - E-Commerce Functionality

8. **Testing and Launch**
   - Steps for Website Testing
   - Pre-Launch Checklist

9. **Maintenance and Updates**
   - Regular Updates and Security Measures
   - Performance Monitoring

10. **Conclusion**
    - Measuring Website Success
    - Future Planning

1.Introduction

Importance of a Website

In today's digital world, having a website is crucial for individuals and businesses alike. A website serves as an online presence that provides information, connects with audiences, and creates opportunities. Here's why having a website is so important:

1. **Online Visibility**: A website acts as a digital storefront. It makes you or your business visible to a global audience. Without a website, you might miss out on reaching potential customers who search for products or services online. It's like having a physical store that's open 24/7, accessible to anyone, anywhere.

2. **Credibility and Professionalism**: In the modern market, a well-designed website adds credibility to your brand. People often judge

a business by its online presence. A professional-looking website can create a positive impression and build trust with your audience. It shows that you're serious and invested in your business.

3. **Information Sharing**: A website is an effective platform for sharing information about your products, services, or personal interests. You can provide detailed descriptions, images, and updates. This allows visitors to learn about what you offer at their own pace, rather than relying on limited social media posts or word of mouth.

4. **Marketing and Advertising**: Websites are essential for online marketing strategies. They allow you to implement SEO (Search Engine Optimization) techniques to rank higher on search engines like Google. This increases the chances of attracting new visitors. Additionally, you can use your website for various advertising campaigns and promotions.

5. **Customer Engagement**: A website can offer interactive features like contact forms, surveys, and chat support, which help engage with visitors and gather feedback. This interaction is valuable for improving customer service and understanding your audience's needs and preferences.

6. **Sales and E-Commerce**: For businesses, a website can be a powerful sales tool. An e-commerce website allows you to sell products or services directly online, reaching customers beyond your local area. It provides a platform for transactions and can handle payments securely.

7. **Analytics and Insights**: Websites offer tools to track visitor behavior through analytics. You can see how many people visit your site, which pages they view, and how they found you. This data helps in making informed decisions to improve your website's performance and marketing strategies.

8. **Competitive Advantage**: Having a website can give you a competitive edge. If your competitors have websites and you don't, they might capture the market share that could have been yours. A website helps you stay relevant and competitive in your industry.

9. **Showcasing Your Work**: For professionals, such as freelancers or artists, a website serves as an online portfolio. It allows you to showcase your work, achievements, and skills. This is crucial for attracting potential clients and employers.

10. **Accessibility**: A website makes your information accessible at any time. Unlike physical stores or offices, your website can be visited by anyone around the clock. This ensures that your audience can find information about you whenever they need it.

In summary, a website is a vital tool for establishing an online presence, enhancing credibility, and engaging with your audience. It supports various business and personal goals by providing information, facilitating communication, and enabling sales. In today's digital age, having a website is not just an option but a necessity for success.

Necessity of Building a Website

In today's digital age, building a website is more important than ever. Here's why having a website is a necessity for individuals and businesses:

1. **Establishing Online Presence**: A website acts as your online identity. Whether you are a business owner, a freelancer, or an individual, having a website allows you to be found on the internet. Without a website, you risk being invisible to potential clients, customers, or even employers who search online for information related to you.

2. **Building Credibility**: A professional website can greatly enhance your credibility. It shows that you are serious about your business or personal brand. When people see a well-designed website, they perceive you as more trustworthy and reliable. This is especially important in a world where online scams and misinformation are prevalent.

3. **Reaching a Wider Audience**: Unlike physical stores or offices, a website can reach a global audience. It allows you to connect with people from different locations and time zones. This broadens your market and increases your chances of finding new customers or clients.

4. **Showcasing Products and Services**: A website provides a platform to showcase what you offer. You can present detailed information about your products or services, including prices, features, and benefits. This helps potential customers understand what you offer and why they should choose you over competitors.

5. **Enhancing Communication**: Websites offer various ways to communicate with your audience. Contact forms, live chat, and email links make it easy for visitors to get in touch with you. This improves customer service and helps you address inquiries, complaints, or feedback efficiently.

6. **Supporting Marketing Efforts**: A website is a crucial component of online marketing strategies. It allows you to implement SEO (Search Engine Optimization) techniques to improve your search engine rankings. Additionally, you can use your website for content marketing, such as blogging, which attracts and engages visitors.

7. **Generating Leads and Sales**: For businesses, a website is essential for generating leads and sales. An e-commerce website allows customers to browse and purchase products online, often with minimal effort. Even if you don't sell directly online, a website can capture leads through forms and calls to action.

8. **Providing Information and Updates**: A website allows you to share important information and updates with your audience. You can post news, events, and announcements that keep your visitors informed. This is especially useful for businesses that need to communicate changes or promotions regularly.

9. **Building Brand Identity**: A website helps in building and reinforcing your brand identity. Through consistent design, messaging, and content,

you can create a strong brand presence. This helps in establishing a clear and memorable image in the minds of your audience.

10. **Collecting Data and Insights**: Websites provide tools to track visitor behavior and gather data. You can analyze how visitors interact with your site, which pages they visit, and how they found you. This information is valuable for improving your website and making data-driven decisions.

In conclusion, building a website is essential in today's digital world. It establishes your online presence, builds credibility, and expands your reach. It supports marketing efforts, enhances communication, and provides a platform for showcasing products or services. Whether for personal or business use, a website is a vital tool for success and growth.

2. Planning and Strategy

Defining Goals and Objectives

Defining goals and objectives is a crucial step in any project or business plan. It involves setting clear, specific targets that guide your efforts and help you measure success. Here's why it's important and how you can do it effectively:

1. **Understanding Goals and Objectives**:
   - **Goals** are broad, overarching outcomes you want to achieve. They represent the end result or the big picture. For instance, a goal might be "to increase website traffic."
   - **Objectives** are specific, measurable actions that help you achieve your goals. They break down the broader goal into manageable steps. For example, an objective might be "to increase website traffic by 20% in six months."

2. **Importance of Setting Goals and Objectives**:
   - **Direction**: Goals and objectives provide a clear direction for your efforts. They act as a roadmap, helping you stay focused and organized. Without them, you might struggle with uncertainty and lack of purpose.
   - **Motivation**: Setting goals gives you something to strive for. It keeps you motivated and encourages you to work towards achieving them. Objectives provide smaller milestones, which can make the process less overwhelming and more achievable.
   - **Measurement**: Defining objectives allows you to measure progress and success. By setting specific, measurable targets, you can track your achievements and make necessary adjustments. This helps in evaluating the effectiveness of your strategies.

3. **How to Define Effective Goals and Objectives**:
   - **Be Specific**: Clearly define what you want to achieve. Avoid vague statements. Instead of saying "improve sales," specify "increase sales by 15% within the next quarter."
   - **Make Them Measurable**: Set criteria that allow you to measure your progress. This could be through numbers, percentages, or specific deadlines. For example, "gain 1,000 new email subscribers in three months" is a measurable objective.
   - **Ensure They Are Achievable**: Goals and objectives should be realistic and attainable. Setting an overly ambitious goal can lead to frustration. Evaluate your resources and capabilities to set achievable targets.
   - **Relevance**: Make sure your goals and objectives are relevant to your overall mission or vision. They should align with your long-term plans and contribute to your overall success.
   - **Set Timeframes**: Assign deadlines or timeframes to your objectives. This creates a sense of urgency and helps in planning your actions. For example, "launch the new website by the end of the month" provides a clear timeline.

4. **Examples of Goals and Objectives**:
   - **Goal**: Improve customer satisfaction.

- **Objective**: Increase the average customer satisfaction score from 80% to 90% within six months by implementing a new feedback system and training staff.
   - **Goal**: Enhance online presence.
   - **Objective**: Boost social media followers by 30% over the next three months by posting daily content and engaging with followers.

5. **Review and Adjust**: Regularly review your goals and objectives to ensure they are still relevant and achievable. Adjust them if necessary based on your progress and any changes in your circumstances or priorities.

In summary, defining clear goals and objectives is essential for guiding your efforts and measuring success. By being specific, measurable, achievable, relevant, and time-bound, you create a structured plan that helps you stay focused and motivated. This process is vital for achieving your desired outcomes and ensuring that your efforts are productive and aligned with your overall vision.

Analyzing Target Audience

Analyzing your target audience is a crucial step in any marketing or business strategy. It involves understanding who your ideal customers are, what they need, and how they behave. Here's why it's important and how you can do it effectively:

1. **Understanding the Target Audience**:
   - **Target Audience**: This refers to the specific group of people or businesses that are most likely to be interested in your products or services. Identifying this group helps you tailor your marketing efforts to reach those who are most likely to convert into customers.

2. **Why It's Important**:
   - **Effective Marketing**: Knowing your target audience allows you to create more relevant and appealing marketing messages. It helps you

focus your resources on the people who are most likely to respond to your offers.
   - **Product Development**: Understanding your audience's needs and preferences helps you develop products or services that meet their demands. This increases the likelihood of success and customer satisfaction.
   - **Improved Communication**: When you know your audience, you can choose the right communication channels and messaging that resonate with them. This ensures that your message reaches them effectively and encourages engagement.

3. **Steps to Analyze Your Target Audience**:
   - **Gather Demographic Information**: Start by collecting basic demographic data such as age, gender, location, income level, and education. This information helps you understand who your audience is at a broad level. For instance, if you sell luxury goods, you might target higher-income individuals.
   - **Identify Psychographic Details**: Go beyond demographics to understand your audience's interests, values, lifestyle, and behaviors. This helps in creating a more detailed profile. For example, if your audience values eco-friendliness, you might highlight the sustainable aspects of your products.
   - **Analyze Behavioral Patterns**: Look at how your audience interacts with your products or services. This includes purchasing habits, online behavior, and brand loyalty. Analyzing these patterns helps in predicting future behavior and refining your marketing strategies.
   - **Conduct Market Research**: Use surveys, interviews, and focus groups to gather insights directly from your audience. This qualitative data provides deeper understanding and helps you address specific needs and concerns.
   - **Monitor Competitors**: Study your competitors to see who their target audience is and how they engage with them. This can reveal market trends and gaps that you can capitalize on.

4. **Creating Customer Profiles**:
   - **Buyer Personas**: Develop detailed profiles or personas representing different segments of your target audience. Each persona should include demographic details, interests, pain points, and

purchasing behavior. This makes it easier to visualize and understand your audience.
   - **Segmentation**: Divide your target audience into smaller, more specific segments based on similar characteristics. For example, you might have different segments for young professionals and retirees if you're marketing a financial planning service.

5. **Applying Audience Insights**:
   - **Tailor Your Marketing**: Use the insights gained from analyzing your audience to create targeted marketing campaigns. This could involve personalized email content, specific social media ads, or tailored product recommendations.
   - **Enhance Product Offerings**: Adjust your products or services based on what you've learned about your audience's needs and preferences. This might involve adding new features or changing how you package your offerings.
   - **Optimize Communication Channels**: Choose the best channels to reach your audience, whether it's social media, email, or traditional advertising. Ensure that your messaging aligns with their preferences and habits.

In summary, analyzing your target audience is essential for effective marketing and business success. By understanding who your audience is, what they need, and how they behave, you can create more relevant strategies, develop better products, and communicate more effectively. This process helps ensure that your efforts are focused and impactful, leading to better outcomes and higher satisfaction.

3.Domain and Hosting

Choosing a Domain Name

Choosing the right domain name is a critical step in building a website. Your domain name is your website's address on the internet, and it plays a significant role in your online presence. Here's how to choose a domain name effectively and why it's important:

1. **What is a Domain Name?**
   - A domain name is the web address people type into their browsers to visit your website, like "www.example.com." It's how users find you online and often forms the first impression of your brand or business.

2. **Why Choosing the Right Domain Name Matters**:
   - **First Impressions**: Your domain name is often the first thing people see about your website. A strong, memorable domain name can create a positive first impression and encourage people to visit your site.
   - **Branding**: A domain name that reflects your brand or business name strengthens your branding. It helps in making your website easily recognizable and associated with your products or services.
   - **SEO Benefits**: A well-chosen domain name can improve your website's search engine optimization (SEO). If your domain name includes relevant keywords, it may help your site rank higher in search engine results, making it easier for people to find you.
   - **Trust and Credibility**: A professional domain name can enhance your credibility. People are more likely to trust and engage with a website that has a strong, professional-sounding domain name.

3. **Tips for Choosing a Domain Name**:
   - **Keep It Simple and Short**: Aim for a domain name that is easy to type, spell, and remember. Shorter domain names are generally better because they are easier to recall and less prone to typos. Avoid complex words or phrases that might confuse users.
   - **Use Keywords Wisely**: If possible, include relevant keywords related to your business or industry. For example, if you run a bakery, including the word "bakery" in your domain name can be beneficial. However, don't force keywords in; the name should still be natural and easy to say.
   - **Choose the Right Domain Extension**: The most common domain extension is ".com," and it's generally the best choice because it's familiar and widely recognized. However, other extensions like ".net," ".org," or country-specific ones like ".in" (for India) can also be used, especially if the ".com" version is unavailable.

- **Avoid Numbers and Hyphens**: Numbers and hyphens can be confusing and hard to remember. People might not know whether to spell out numbers or use numerals, and hyphens are often forgotten, leading to lost traffic.
- **Make It Brandable**: Your domain name should be unique and reflect your brand. Avoid using generic terms that don't stand out. A brandable name is one that is distinctive, memorable, and easy to associate with your business.
- **Think Long-Term**: Choose a domain name that can grow with your business. Avoid names that are too specific to a particular product or service if you plan to expand your offerings in the future. A flexible domain name allows your brand to evolve without needing a complete rebranding.
- **Check for Availability**: Before finalizing your domain name, check to ensure it's available. You can use domain registration sites to see if the name is already taken. Also, check social media platforms to secure consistent usernames for your brand.
- **Consider Legal Implications**: Make sure your chosen domain name doesn't infringe on any trademarks or copyrights. This can prevent legal issues down the road and protect your brand.

4. **Registering Your Domain Name**:
   - Once you've chosen a domain name, you need to register it with a domain registrar. Popular registrars include GoDaddy, Namecheap, and Google Domains. Registration usually involves an annual fee, and it's wise to register your domain for multiple years to secure it long-term.

5. **Conclusion**:
   - Choosing the right domain name is a vital part of creating a successful website. It impacts your branding, SEO, and the overall perception of your site. By keeping it simple, relevant, and memorable, you can ensure that your domain name effectively supports your online presence and helps you build a strong, recognizable brand. Remember to think long-term and consider the future growth of your business when making your choice.

Types of Web Hosting

When you build a website, one of the important decisions you need to make is choosing the right type of web hosting. Web hosting is the service that allows your website to be accessible on the internet. Different types of web hosting offer varying levels of control, performance, and cost. Here's an explanation of the main types of web hosting, explained in simple language:

1. **Shared Hosting**:
   - **What It Is**: Shared hosting is like renting an apartment in a large building. Your website shares server resources (like CPU, memory, and bandwidth) with many other websites. It's the most common and affordable type of hosting.
   - **Pros**: The main advantage of shared hosting is its low cost, making it a good option for beginners or small websites that don't need a lot of resources. It's also easy to set up and manage, with most of the technical work handled by the hosting provider.
   - **Cons**: Because you share resources with other websites, your site's performance can be affected if another site on the same server experiences high traffic. You also have limited control over the server's configuration.

2. **VPS (Virtual Private Server) Hosting**:
   - **What It Is**: VPS hosting is like owning a condo in a larger building. You still share the physical server with others, but you have your own dedicated portion of the server's resources. It's more powerful and flexible than shared hosting.
   - **Pros**: With VPS hosting, you get more control over your server environment. You can install custom software and have more resources dedicated to your site, which improves performance. It's a good option for growing websites that need more power than shared hosting but don't require a full server.
   - **Cons**: VPS hosting is more expensive than shared hosting. It also requires more technical knowledge to manage, although some providers offer managed VPS services where they handle the technical aspects for you.

3. **Dedicated Hosting**:
   - **What It Is**: Dedicated hosting is like owning your own house. You have an entire physical server dedicated to your website. This means you have full control over the server's resources and configuration.
   - **Pros**: Dedicated hosting offers the highest level of performance and security. You have complete control over how the server is set up and can customize it to meet your specific needs. It's ideal for large websites with high traffic or those requiring strict security measures.
   - **Cons**: This is the most expensive type of hosting. It also requires a high level of technical expertise to manage, as you're responsible for maintaining the server.

4. **Cloud Hosting**:
   - **What It Is**: Cloud hosting is like living in a network of connected houses, where resources are spread across multiple servers. Your website doesn't rely on a single server but instead uses a network of servers, or "the cloud."
   - **Pros**: Cloud hosting offers great flexibility and scalability. You can easily increase or decrease your resources based on your website's needs. It's also very reliable because if one server fails, another can take over, minimizing downtime.
   - **Cons**: Cloud hosting can be more complex and costly than shared or VPS hosting. Costs can also vary depending on how much you use, making it harder to predict expenses.

5. **Managed Hosting**:
   - **What It Is**: Managed hosting can be any of the hosting types mentioned above (shared, VPS, or dedicated) but with an added service layer where the hosting provider manages all the technical aspects for you.
   - **Pros**: Managed hosting takes the burden of server management off your shoulders. The hosting provider handles everything from security updates to backups and monitoring. It's ideal for businesses or individuals who want to focus on running their website without worrying about the technical details.

- **Cons**: Managed hosting is usually more expensive than unmanaged options. You also have less control over the server's configuration since the hosting provider manages it.

6. **WordPress Hosting**:
   - **What It Is**: WordPress hosting is specifically optimized for WordPress websites. It can be shared, VPS, or dedicated, but it's configured to offer the best performance, security, and features for WordPress users.
   - **Pros**: WordPress hosting comes with pre-installed WordPress, automatic updates, and specialized support. It's an excellent choice for beginners or those who want to run a WordPress site with minimal hassle.
   - **Cons**: It may be more expensive than regular shared hosting, and it's not suitable if you want to use another content management system besides WordPress.

In conclusion, the type of web hosting you choose depends on your website's needs, budget, and technical expertise. Shared hosting is a good starting point for small websites, while VPS and dedicated hosting offer more power and control for growing sites. Cloud hosting provides flexibility and reliability, and managed hosting takes care of the technical details for you. By understanding these options, you can choose the best hosting solution for your website.

4. Website Design

Principles of User-Friendly Design

User-friendly design is all about making websites and applications easy and enjoyable for people to use. Whether you're creating a website, app, or any other digital product, following the principles of user-friendly design can ensure that your users have a positive experience. Here are the key principles explained in simple language:

1. **Simplicity**:
   - **Keep It Simple**: Simplicity is the cornerstone of user-friendly design. Your design should be straightforward, with no unnecessary elements that could confuse users. This means using a clean layout, minimal text, and only essential features. For example, instead of cluttering a page with too many buttons and links, focus on the most important actions you want users to take.
   - **Easy Navigation**: Your users should be able to find what they're looking for quickly and easily. This means having a clear and intuitive menu, organized content, and a search function if necessary. Navigation should be consistent across all pages, so users always know where they are and how to get back to the homepage.

2. **Clarity**:
   - **Make It Clear**: Users should never be confused about what something means on your website or app. Use simple and familiar language, and avoid jargon or technical terms that might be hard to understand. Clear labels on buttons, straightforward instructions, and a logical layout help users know exactly what to do.
   - **Visual Hierarchy**: Arrange elements in a way that guides users' attention to the most important information first. Use different sizes, colors, and placements to show what's most important. For example, a "Buy Now" button might be larger and more brightly colored than other buttons to stand out.

3. **Consistency**:
   - **Uniform Design**: Consistency means that everything in your design follows the same style and structure. This includes fonts, colors, button styles, and how different elements behave. For instance, if clicking a button takes users to a new page in one part of your website, it should do the same in all other parts. Consistency helps users feel comfortable and confident because they know what to expect.
   - **Predictable Behavior**: Ensure that actions on your site or app behave the way users expect. For example, clicking on a logo typically takes users to the homepage, and links usually change color after being clicked. Keeping these behaviors consistent across your design builds trust and reduces confusion.

4. **Feedback**:
   - **Instant Feedback**: Provide users with immediate feedback for their actions. If they click a button, submit a form, or hover over a link, there should be a visual or auditory response. For example, a button might change color when clicked, or a loading spinner might appear while a page is loading. This feedback reassures users that the system is working and responding to their input.
   - **Error Messages**: When something goes wrong, clear and helpful error messages should guide users on what to do next. Instead of saying "Error 404," a message like "Sorry, the page you're looking for isn't here. Try searching or go back to the homepage" is more user-friendly.

5. **Accessibility**:
   - **Inclusive Design**: Your design should be accessible to everyone, including people with disabilities. This means using high-contrast colors for text, providing text alternatives for images (like alt text), and ensuring that your site is navigable with a keyboard, not just a mouse. An accessible design ensures that all users, regardless of their abilities, can interact with your site effectively.
   - **Responsive Design**: Your website or app should work well on all devices, whether it's a desktop, tablet, or smartphone. Responsive design automatically adjusts the layout to fit the screen size, making it easier for users to navigate and read content on any device.

6. **User Control**:
   - **Empower Users**: Give users control over their experience. This includes options to undo actions, customize their settings, and easily navigate backward and forward. For example, if a user accidentally deletes something, there should be an easy way to recover it. Giving users control helps them feel more confident and in charge of their experience.

7. **Efficiency**:
   - **Speed and Performance**: A user-friendly design ensures that your website or app loads quickly and runs smoothly. Users don't want to wait for slow pages to load or deal with laggy interactions. Optimize images, minimize code, and use efficient hosting to keep your site running fast.

- **Task Efficiency**: Design your site so that users can complete their tasks with minimal effort. This might involve simplifying forms, reducing the number of steps needed to purchase a product, or providing quick access to frequently used features.

In summary, the principles of user-friendly design revolve around simplicity, clarity, consistency, feedback, accessibility, user control, and efficiency. By focusing on these principles, you create a design that is not only easy to use but also enjoyable, ensuring that users have a positive experience every time they interact with your website or app. A user-friendly design leads to satisfied users, which can translate into more engagement, loyalty, and success for your digital product.

Importance of Responsive Design

Responsive design is a crucial aspect of modern web development. It ensures that a website looks and functions well on all devices, whether it's a desktop computer, tablet, or smartphone. With the increasing variety of devices people use to access the internet, having a responsive design has become more important than ever. Here's why responsive design is essential, explained in simple terms:

1. **Adapting to Different Screen Sizes**:
   - **One Website, Many Devices**: A responsive design automatically adjusts to fit the screen size of any device. Whether someone is viewing your website on a large desktop monitor or a small smartphone screen, the layout, images, and text will resize and rearrange to provide the best possible user experience. This adaptability is key because it ensures that your website is accessible and easy to use on any device.

2. **Improving User Experience**:
   - **Ease of Navigation**: A responsive website is easy to navigate, no matter what device it's viewed on. For example, on a smartphone, menus might become dropdowns to save space, and buttons might be larger to make them easier to tap. By making your website user-friendly

across all devices, you improve the overall experience for your visitors, which can lead to higher engagement and satisfaction.
   - **Consistent Look and Feel**: With responsive design, your website maintains a consistent look and feel across all devices. This consistency helps build trust with your users, as they know what to expect when they visit your site, whether they're on their phone, tablet, or computer.

3. **Boosting SEO (Search Engine Optimization)**:
   - **Google's Preference**: Search engines like Google prioritize mobile-friendly websites in their search results. This means that if your website is responsive, it's more likely to rank higher in search results, making it easier for people to find you online. A higher ranking can lead to more visitors and potential customers.
   - **Single URL**: With responsive design, you only need one version of your website for all devices. This means that all your traffic is directed to a single URL, which is beneficial for SEO. It also simplifies the management of your website, as you don't need to maintain separate versions for mobile and desktop.

4. **Cost-Effective and Time-Saving**:
   - **One Design, Multiple Devices**: Developing a responsive website is more cost-effective and time-efficient than creating separate websites for different devices. With responsive design, you only need to design and develop one site that works everywhere. This reduces the time and effort needed for updates and maintenance, saving you money in the long run.
   - **Future-Proofing**: As new devices with different screen sizes continue to emerge, a responsive website is better equipped to handle these changes. Instead of redesigning your website for each new device, a responsive design automatically adapts, making it a more sustainable solution.

5. **Increasing Conversion Rates**:
   - **More Sales and Leads**: A responsive website can lead to higher conversion rates, meaning more visitors take desired actions like making a purchase or filling out a contact form. When users can easily navigate your site and find what they're looking for, they're more likely to become

customers. If your site isn't responsive, users might become frustrated and leave, leading to lost opportunities.
   - **Better Engagement**: A responsive design encourages users to spend more time on your website, exploring your content and services. The longer they stay, the more likely they are to engage with your site, whether that's through reading blog posts, watching videos, or making a purchase.

6. **Catering to Mobile Users**:
   - **Mobile Traffic**: With more people accessing the internet via smartphones and tablets than ever before, it's essential to cater to mobile users. A responsive design ensures that mobile visitors have a seamless experience, without the need for zooming, scrolling, or dealing with tiny buttons. This is especially important for businesses, as mobile users are often on the go and looking for quick, easy access to information or services.
   - **Meeting User Expectations**: Today's users expect websites to be mobile-friendly. If your site isn't responsive, visitors may see it as outdated or difficult to use, which can harm your brand's reputation. By meeting or exceeding user expectations with a responsive design, you can build trust and encourage repeat visits.

7. **Staying Competitive**:
   - **Keeping Up with Trends**: As more websites adopt responsive design, it has become the industry standard. To stay competitive, especially in crowded markets, it's crucial to have a website that's as accessible and user-friendly as your competitors'. A responsive design ensures that you're not left behind as more businesses and individuals prioritize mobile-friendly websites.

In conclusion, responsive design is essential for ensuring that your website provides a positive experience for all users, regardless of the device they're using. It enhances user experience, improves SEO, saves time and money, and helps you stay competitive. By adopting a responsive design, you can ensure that your website is well-equipped to handle the diverse ways people access the internet today and in the future.

5. Content Creation

Creating High-Quality Content

Creating high-quality content is one of the most important aspects of building a successful website. Whether you're writing blog posts, creating videos, or sharing images, the quality of your content directly impacts how visitors perceive your site and how well it performs in search engines. Here's why high-quality content is crucial and how to create it, explained in simple terms.

1. **Engaging Your Audience**:
   - **Meeting User Needs**: High-quality content is content that meets the needs and interests of your audience. This means understanding what your visitors are looking for and providing them with valuable, relevant information. When your content answers their questions, solves their problems, or entertains them, they are more likely to stay on your site longer, explore more pages, and return in the future.
   - **Clear and Concise**: To engage your audience effectively, your content should be clear, concise, and easy to understand. Avoid using complex language or jargon that might confuse your readers. Instead, aim to communicate your message in a straightforward and simple manner. This makes your content accessible to a wider audience and keeps readers interested.

2. **Building Trust and Authority**:
   - **Accuracy and Reliability**: High-quality content is accurate and well-researched. Providing reliable information helps build trust with your audience. When visitors see that your content is well-informed and fact-checked, they are more likely to view your site as a credible source. This trust can lead to higher engagement, more shares, and even conversions, such as sales or sign-ups.

- **Expertise and Authority**: Creating content that demonstrates your expertise in a particular field helps establish your authority. For example, if you run a health blog, sharing in-depth articles backed by scientific research can position you as an expert in that area. When users perceive you as an authority, they are more likely to return to your site and recommend it to others.

3. **Improving Search Engine Rankings**:
   - **SEO Benefits**: High-quality content is a key factor in search engine optimization (SEO). Search engines like Google prioritize content that is original, informative, and valuable to users. When you consistently produce high-quality content, your site is more likely to rank higher in search results, making it easier for people to find you online. This can lead to increased traffic and visibility for your site.
   - **Keyword Optimization**: While creating content, it's important to incorporate relevant keywords naturally. These are the words and phrases that people use when searching for information related to your topic. However, avoid "keyword stuffing," which means overloading your content with keywords in an unnatural way. Focus on creating content that flows naturally while still including important keywords.

4. **Encouraging Social Sharing**:
   - **Shareable Content**: High-quality content is often shared on social media, helping to increase your reach and drive more traffic to your site. When people find your content valuable or interesting, they are more likely to share it with their friends, family, and followers. To make your content more shareable, include eye-catching images, compelling headlines, and share buttons that make it easy for users to spread the word.
   - **Creating Emotional Connections**: Content that resonates with people on an emotional level is more likely to be shared. Whether it's content that makes them laugh, think, or feel inspired, creating an emotional connection can encourage users to share your content. This not only increases your visibility but also helps build a community around your brand or message.

5. **Driving Conversions**:

- **Call to Action**: High-quality content can help drive conversions by including clear calls to action (CTAs). A CTA prompts users to take a specific action, such as signing up for a newsletter, making a purchase, or downloading a free guide. When your content is engaging and persuasive, users are more likely to respond to these CTAs, leading to higher conversion rates.
   - **Content That Solves Problems**: If your content addresses common problems or challenges that your audience faces, it can guide them toward taking action. For example, a blog post about choosing the right product might include a CTA to check out your online store. By providing solutions through your content, you can encourage users to take the next step in their journey with your brand.

6. **Consistency and Frequency**:
   - **Regular Updates**: Consistently creating and publishing high-quality content helps keep your audience engaged and coming back for more. Whether it's a weekly blog post, a monthly newsletter, or daily social media updates, maintaining a regular content schedule shows that your site is active and up-to-date. It also helps improve your SEO, as search engines favor sites that are frequently updated with fresh content.
   - **Quality Over Quantity**: While it's important to post regularly, quality should always come first. It's better to produce fewer pieces of high-quality content than to churn out a large volume of mediocre content. High-quality content is more likely to resonate with your audience, attract attention, and achieve your goals.

7. **Adapting to Different Formats**:
   - **Diverse Content Types**: High-quality content comes in many forms, including blog posts, videos, infographics, podcasts, and more. Adapting your content to different formats can help you reach a broader audience. For example, some people prefer reading articles, while others might enjoy watching videos or listening to podcasts. By offering a variety of content types, you can cater to different preferences and increase your overall reach.
   - **Mobile-Friendly Content**: As more people access content on their smartphones and tablets, it's important to ensure that your content is mobile-friendly. This means that your text, images, and videos should be

easy to view and interact with on smaller screens. Mobile-friendly content is more likely to be consumed and shared, contributing to the overall success of your site.

In conclusion, creating high-quality content is essential for engaging your audience, building trust, improving SEO, encouraging social sharing, driving conversions, and maintaining consistency. By focusing on quality over quantity and adapting to different formats, you can create content that resonates with your audience and helps achieve your website's goals.

SEO-Friendly Content

SEO (Search Engine Optimization) is a strategy used to increase the visibility of a website on search engines like Google. When you create SEO-friendly content, you're essentially making it easier for search engines to understand and rank your content, which can lead to higher placement in search results. This, in turn, helps more people find your website. Here's how to create SEO-friendly content, explained in simple terms:

1. **Understanding Keywords**:
   - **What Are Keywords?**: Keywords are the words and phrases that people type into search engines when looking for information. For example, if someone is searching for tips on gardening, they might use keywords like "gardening tips," "how to grow plants," or "best gardening tools."
   - **Choosing the Right Keywords**: To create SEO-friendly content, start by choosing the right keywords that are relevant to your topic. These should be terms that people are likely to search for. You can use tools like Google Keyword Planner or Ubersuggest to find popular keywords related to your subject.
   - **Using Keywords Effectively**: Once you've identified your keywords, use them naturally in your content. This means including them in the title, headings, and throughout the body of your text. However,

avoid "keyword stuffing," which is the practice of overusing keywords to manipulate search rankings. This can actually hurt your SEO. The key is to use keywords in a way that feels natural and flows well within the content.

2. **Creating High-Quality Content**:
   - **Focus on the User**: SEO-friendly content isn't just about keywords; it's also about providing value to your readers. Search engines prioritize content that is informative, useful, and relevant to the user's search query. When creating content, think about what your audience wants to know and how you can help them.
   - **Longer Content Is Often Better**: Longer, in-depth content tends to perform better in search engines because it provides more information and value to the reader. Aim for content that is at least 1,000 words long, but don't add unnecessary information just to reach a word count. The content should be thorough and relevant.
   - **Keep It Readable**: High-quality content is also easy to read. Break up long paragraphs, use bullet points and subheadings, and write in short, clear sentences. This not only makes the content more engaging for readers but also makes it easier for search engines to understand and rank your content.

3. **Optimizing Meta Tags**:
   - **Title Tags**: The title tag is the main headline that appears in search engine results. It should be clear, include your primary keyword, and be compelling enough to make people want to click on it. A good title tag is usually around 50-60 characters long.
   - **Meta Descriptions**: The meta description is the short summary that appears below the title in search results. While it doesn't directly affect your rankings, it can influence whether people click on your link. A good meta description should be around 150-160 characters long, include your main keyword, and give a brief but enticing overview of what the content is about.
   - **Alt Text for Images**: Alt text is a description of an image that helps search engines understand what the image is about. Including alt text with your images can improve your SEO and make your content more accessible to people using screen readers. Be sure to use relevant keywords in your alt text, but keep the description accurate and concise.

4. **Using Internal and External Links**:
   - **Internal Links**: These are links that point to other pages on your own website. Internal links help search engines understand the structure of your site and can keep visitors on your site longer by guiding them to additional content. When adding internal links, use descriptive anchor text (the clickable text in a hyperlink) that includes relevant keywords.
   - **External Links**: These are links that point to other websites. External links to high-quality, authoritative sites can enhance the credibility of your own content. It shows search engines that you're providing valuable information that's well-supported by other trusted sources. Just be sure to link to reliable and relevant websites.

5. **Making Content Shareable**:
   - **Encourage Social Sharing**: Content that is shared on social media can drive traffic to your site and improve your SEO. Include social sharing buttons on your website to make it easy for visitors to share your content. When your content is shared, it signals to search engines that it's valuable and relevant, which can help boost your rankings.
   - **Create Engaging Content**: The more engaging and informative your content is, the more likely people are to share it. Use images, videos, and infographics to make your content more appealing. Engaging content not only attracts readers but also encourages them to share it with others, expanding your reach and potential audience.

6. **Optimizing for Mobile**:
   - **Mobile-Friendly Content**: With more people using smartphones to browse the internet, it's essential that your content is mobile-friendly. Search engines like Google prioritize mobile-friendly websites, so if your content isn't optimized for mobile, you could be missing out on potential visitors.
   - **Responsive Design**: Make sure your website uses responsive design, which automatically adjusts the layout of your content to fit different screen sizes. This ensures that your content is easy to read and navigate, whether visitors are using a desktop computer, tablet, or smartphone.

7. **Regularly Updating Content**:

- **Fresh Content**: Search engines favor websites that regularly update their content. This doesn't mean you need to create new content every day, but you should periodically review and update existing content to keep it fresh and relevant. Updating content can include adding new information, refreshing old data, or improving readability.
- **Reposting and Repurposing**: If you have content that performed well in the past, consider repurposing it into a different format, like turning a blog post into a video or infographic. Reposting updated content can also help it reach new audiences and improve its visibility in search engines.

In conclusion, creating SEO-friendly content involves understanding and using keywords effectively, producing high-quality and readable content, optimizing meta tags, using internal and external links, making content shareable, ensuring it's mobile-friendly, and regularly updating it. By following these practices, you can improve your website's visibility, attract more visitors, and achieve better rankings on search engines.

6. Development Tools and Platforms

Website Builders vs. Custom Development

When it comes to creating a website, you have two main options: using a website builder or opting for custom development. Both approaches have their own advantages and challenges, depending on your needs, technical skills, and budget. Here's a breakdown of the differences between website builders and custom development, explained in simple terms.

Website Builders

1. **What Are Website Builders?**
   - **Definition**: Website builders are online platforms that allow you to create a website without needing to write any code. They offer drag-and-drop interfaces, templates, and pre-built design elements, making it easy for anyone to build a website.
   - **Examples**: Popular website builders include Wix, Squarespace, Weebly, and WordPress.com.

2. **Advantages of Website Builders**:
   - **Ease of Use**: Website builders are designed for simplicity. You don't need any technical knowledge or coding skills to create a website. The drag-and-drop functionality allows you to customize your site by simply moving elements around, choosing colors, and adding content.
   - **Quick Setup**: With a website builder, you can have your website up and running in a matter of hours. Most builders offer ready-made templates that you can modify to suit your needs, which speeds up the process.
   - **Cost-Effective**: Website builders are generally more affordable than custom development. They often come with hosting, security, and support included in the price, making them a budget-friendly option for individuals and small businesses.
   - **All-in-One Solution**: Website builders often include everything you need in one package, such as hosting, domain registration, and customer support. This simplifies the process of managing your website, as you don't need to deal with multiple providers.

3. **Challenges of Website Builders**:
   - **Limited Customization**: While website builders offer plenty of templates and customization options, they have limitations. You may not be able to achieve a unique design or specific functionality that you could with custom development.
   - **Scalability Issues**: Website builders are great for small to medium-sized websites, but they may struggle to handle large-scale or highly complex sites. If your website grows significantly, you may outgrow the capabilities of the builder.

- **Less Control**: With a website builder, you're limited to the features and design options provided by the platform. This means you have less control over the finer details of your website compared to custom development.

Custom Development

1. **What Is Custom Development?**
   - **Definition**: Custom development involves building a website from scratch using coding languages like HTML, CSS, JavaScript, and frameworks such as React or Laravel. This approach allows for complete control over the design, functionality, and user experience of the website.
   - **How It Works**: Custom development usually requires hiring a professional developer or a development team to create the website according to your specific requirements.

2. **Advantages of Custom Development**:
   - **Unlimited Customization**: Custom development offers complete flexibility and control over your website's design and functionality. You can create a truly unique site tailored to your exact needs, with custom features and integrations that aren't possible with website builders.
   - **Scalability**: Custom websites are built to grow with your business. As your needs evolve, you can add new features, pages, and functionality without being restricted by the limitations of a website builder.
   - **Enhanced Performance**: Custom websites are often faster and more efficient because they're built with clean, optimized code. Developers can fine-tune the site to ensure it performs well, even as it scales.
   - **Better SEO and Security**: Custom development allows for more advanced SEO strategies and stronger security measures. You have full control over the site's structure, meta tags, and other SEO elements, which can help improve your search engine rankings. Additionally, custom websites can be more secure since you're not relying on third-party platforms that could have vulnerabilities.

3. **Challenges of Custom Development**:

- **Higher Cost**: Custom development is generally more expensive than using a website builder. The cost includes hiring developers, designers, and possibly ongoing maintenance. This makes it a better option for those with a larger budget.
- **Longer Development Time**: Building a custom website takes more time compared to using a website builder. The process involves planning, designing, coding, testing, and launching the site, which can take weeks or even months, depending on the complexity of the project.
- **Requires Technical Knowledge**: While you don't need to be a developer yourself, managing a custom-built website requires some technical understanding. You'll need to work closely with your development team and may need to handle aspects like hosting and updates on your own or through your developers.

Which Option Is Right for You?

1. **Consider Your Needs**: If you need a simple website that's quick to set up, like a personal blog or a small business site, a website builder is a great choice. It's user-friendly, cost-effective, and covers all the basics you'll need.

2. **Think About the Future**: If you anticipate needing a lot of custom features or if your website is central to your business (like an e-commerce store or a large content site), custom development might be worth the investment. It provides the flexibility, scalability, and performance needed for complex sites.

3. **Evaluate Your Budget**: Custom development requires a larger budget, both for the initial build and ongoing maintenance. If you have limited funds, a website builder might be the more practical option.

In conclusion, the choice between a website builder and custom development depends on your specific needs, budget, and future plans. Website builders are ideal for those who want an easy, affordable, and fast solution, while custom development is perfect for those who need a highly customized, scalable, and performance-driven website. Understanding the pros and cons of each option will help you make the best decision for your website project.

Choosing a CMS (Content Management System)

A Content Management System (CMS) is an essential tool for creating, managing, and maintaining a website without needing to have deep technical knowledge. It allows you to organize and publish content, customize the appearance of your site, and manage users, all from a user-friendly interface. Choosing the right CMS is crucial as it can significantly impact your website's functionality, user experience, and scalability. Here's a guide to help you understand what a CMS is, why it's important, and how to choose the best one for your needs.

What is a CMS?

1. **Definition**: A CMS is software that enables you to create, edit, and manage digital content on a website. It separates the content (like text, images, and videos) from the design, allowing you to focus on your content without worrying about coding or technical details.

2. **How It Works**: A CMS typically has two parts:
   - **Content Management Application (CMA)**: This is the part of the CMS that allows you to create and manage content. It provides an easy-to-use interface where you can add text, images, videos, and other media to your website.
   - **Content Delivery Application (CDA)**: This part of the CMS takes the content you create in the CMA and displays it on your website. It handles the behind-the-scenes work of integrating your content with the website's design and structure.

Why Choosing the Right CMS is Important

1. **Ease of Use**: The right CMS should be easy to use, even for beginners. It should allow you to create and manage content without

needing to write code. A user-friendly CMS will save you time and make it easier to keep your website up-to-date.

2. **Customization**: Your CMS should allow you to customize the look and feel of your website. This includes choosing from a variety of themes, templates, and plugins or modules that add functionality. A customizable CMS gives you the flexibility to create a website that reflects your brand and meets your specific needs.

3. **Scalability**: As your website grows, you'll need a CMS that can scale with you. Whether you're adding more content, increasing traffic, or expanding features, the right CMS should be able to handle growth without requiring a complete overhaul.

4. **Support and Community**: A good CMS should have strong support, either through official channels or a large, active community. This is important if you run into issues or need help customizing your site. A CMS with a strong community will have plenty of resources, like tutorials, forums, and plugins, that can help you solve problems and add new features.

Popular CMS Options

1. **WordPress**
   - **Overview**: WordPress is the most popular CMS in the world, powering over 40% of all websites. It's known for its ease of use, extensive customization options, and a large library of plugins and themes.
   - **Best For**: WordPress is ideal for blogs, small businesses, and even large enterprise websites. It's versatile enough to handle a wide range of website types, from simple blogs to complex e-commerce sites.
   - **Advantages**:
     - Easy to use, even for beginners.
     - Extensive library of plugins and themes for customization.
     - Large, active community with plenty of resources.
   - **Challenges**:
     - Requires regular updates and maintenance.

    - Some advanced features may require coding knowledge or hiring a developer.

2. **Joomla**
    - **Overview**: Joomla is a powerful, flexible CMS that's slightly more complex than WordPress. It offers more built-in features, which can be great for users who need more control over their site's functionality.
    - **Best For**: Joomla is suitable for websites that require more complex structures, like online magazines, corporate websites, or social networks.
    - **Advantages**:
      - Offers more built-in features out of the box.
      - Flexible and scalable for more complex websites.
      - Strong community support.
    - **Challenges**:
      - Steeper learning curve compared to WordPress.
      - Not as many themes and plugins available, which may limit customization options.

3. **Drupal**
    - **Overview**: Drupal is a highly customizable, robust CMS that's designed for developers and experienced users. It's known for its strong security, scalability, and ability to handle large amounts of content.
    - **Best For**: Drupal is ideal for large, complex websites with high traffic, like government sites, large corporations, and universities.
    - **Advantages**:
      - Extremely flexible and customizable.
      - Strong security features.
      - Excellent scalability for large websites.
    - **Challenges**:
      - Requires significant technical knowledge.
      - Steep learning curve, especially for beginners.
      - Smaller community compared to WordPress, which may mean fewer resources and support options.

4. **Wix**

- **Overview**: Wix is a cloud-based website builder that also functions as a CMS. It's designed for users who want to create a website quickly and easily without worrying about coding.
- **Best For**: Wix is best for small businesses, portfolios, and personal websites that don't require a lot of complex features.
  - **Advantages**:
    - Very easy to use with a drag-and-drop interface.
    - No coding required.
    - Includes hosting and domain registration.
  - **Challenges**:
    - Limited customization options compared to other CMS platforms.
    - Not as scalable, making it less suitable for larger websites.
    - Fewer plugins and extensions available.

How to Choose the Right CMS

1. **Assess Your Needs**: Start by considering what you need from your website. Are you creating a simple blog, an online store, or a large corporate site? Your requirements will help narrow down the best CMS for you.

2. **Evaluate Ease of Use**: If you're new to website management, choose a CMS that's easy to learn and use. WordPress and Wix are great options for beginners, while Joomla and Drupal may require more technical skills.

3. **Consider Customization and Scalability**: Think about how much control you need over your website's design and functionality. If you need a highly customizable site that can grow with your business, Drupal or Joomla might be the right choice. For simpler needs, WordPress or Wix may suffice.

4. **Look at Support and Community**: Check if the CMS has good support options and an active community. This is important for troubleshooting and finding resources as you build and maintain your website.

5. **Test It Out**: Many CMS platforms offer demos or free trials. Take advantage of these to explore the interface and see if it meets your needs before committing.

In conclusion, choosing the right CMS is crucial for the success of your website. By understanding your needs, considering ease of use, customization, scalability, and support, you can select the CMS that will help you create and manage a website that meets your goals. Whether you choose a popular option like WordPress or a more advanced platform like Drupal, the right CMS will make your website easier to build, manage, and grow.

7.Website Functionality

Essential Features and Plugins for a Website

When creating a website, certain features and plugins are essential to ensure it runs smoothly, offers a good user experience, and meets your business or personal goals. These tools can help improve the functionality, security, and performance of your website, making it more effective in attracting and retaining visitors. Here's a guide to understanding the key features and plugins that every website should have.

1. Essential Website Features

1. **Responsive Design**
   - **Definition**: Responsive design means your website automatically adjusts its layout and content to fit any screen size, whether it's a desktop, tablet, or smartphone.
   - **Importance**: With more people accessing websites on mobile devices, it's crucial that your site looks good and works well on all screen

sizes. A responsive design improves user experience and helps retain visitors.
   - **Implementation**: Most modern website builders and themes are designed to be responsive, but it's always a good idea to test your site on different devices to ensure it works smoothly.

2. **Fast Loading Speed**
   - **Definition**: This refers to how quickly your website's pages load for visitors.
   - **Importance**: A fast-loading website is crucial for keeping users engaged. If your site takes too long to load, visitors might leave before they even see your content. Speed also affects your site's ranking on search engines like Google.
   - **Implementation**: You can improve loading speed by optimizing images, using a Content Delivery Network (CDN), and choosing a reliable hosting service.

3. **User-Friendly Navigation**
   - **Definition**: Navigation refers to how users move through your website using menus, links, and buttons.
   - **Importance**: Clear and simple navigation helps users find the information they need quickly and easily. Good navigation enhances user experience and can lead to higher engagement and conversion rates.
   - **Implementation**: Organize your website's content into categories, use descriptive labels for menu items, and ensure your navigation is consistent across all pages.

4. **Security Features**
   - **Definition**: Security features protect your website from cyber threats like hacking, malware, and data breaches.
   - **Importance**: Security is critical, especially if your website handles sensitive information like customer data or payment details. A secure website builds trust with your visitors and protects your business from legal and financial risks.
   - **Implementation**: Use HTTPS encryption, install security plugins, regularly update your website's software, and use strong passwords.

5. **Search Functionality**
   - **Definition**: This feature allows visitors to search for specific content on your website.
   - **Importance**: A search function is especially important for larger websites with lots of content. It helps users find what they're looking for quickly, improving their overall experience on your site.
   - **Implementation**: Include a search bar in a prominent location on your website, such as the header, and ensure it returns relevant results.

2. Essential Plugins for WordPress Websites

If you're using WordPress, plugins are additional tools that can extend the functionality of your website. Here are some must-have plugins:

1. **Yoast SEO**
   - **Purpose**: Yoast SEO helps optimize your website's content for search engines, improving your chances of ranking higher in search results.
   - **Key Features**: It provides suggestions for improving your content's SEO, such as using the right keywords, optimizing meta descriptions, and ensuring your content is easy to read.
   - **Why It's Essential**: SEO is critical for driving organic traffic to your website. Yoast SEO makes it easier to optimize your site even if you're not an SEO expert.

2. **Wordfence Security**
   - **Purpose**: Wordfence Security protects your website from various security threats, including hacking attempts and malware.
   - **Key Features**: It offers a firewall, malware scanner, and real-time threat detection. It also monitors login attempts and blocks suspicious activity.
   - **Why It's Essential**: Security is a top priority for any website. Wordfence Security provides comprehensive protection, helping to keep your site safe from cyberattacks.

3. **WP Super Cache**

- **Purpose**: WP Super Cache improves your website's loading speed by generating static HTML files and serving them to visitors instead of processing the full WordPress PHP scripts.
- **Key Features**: It reduces server load, speeds up your website, and improves user experience, especially during traffic spikes.
- **Why It's Essential**: Faster loading times lead to better user experience and higher search engine rankings. WP Super Cache is a simple way to boost your website's performance.

4. **Contact Form 7**
   - **Purpose**: Contact Form 7 allows you to create and manage multiple contact forms on your website.
   - **Key Features**: It's easy to use, customizable, and supports various types of forms, such as contact forms, surveys, and feedback forms.
   - **Why It's Essential**: Having a contact form on your website makes it easy for visitors to get in touch with you, whether they have questions, feedback, or business inquiries.

5. **WooCommerce**
   - **Purpose**: WooCommerce is a powerful plugin for creating and managing an online store on your website.
   - **Key Features**: It allows you to sell products, manage inventory, process payments, and handle shipping, all from your WordPress site.
   - **Why It's Essential**: If you plan to sell products or services online, WooCommerce is the go-to solution for turning your WordPress site into a fully functional e-commerce store.

Conclusion

The functionality of your website is not just about making it look good; it's about ensuring it works well and meets the needs of your users. By focusing on essential features like responsive design, fast loading speed, user-friendly navigation, security, and search functionality, you can create a website that provides a great user experience. Additionally, if you're using WordPress, essential plugins like Yoast SEO, Wordfence Security, WP Super Cache, Contact Form 7, and WooCommerce can enhance your site's functionality, making it more secure, faster, and easier to manage. These tools and features are the building blocks of a successful website that attracts visitors, keeps them engaged, and helps you achieve your goals.

E-Commerce Functionality

E-commerce functionality refers to the features and tools that enable an online store to sell products or services effectively. Whether you're running a small shop or a large online marketplace, having the right e-commerce functionality is essential for providing a smooth shopping experience to your customers. This guide will explain the key elements of e-commerce functionality in simple language so that anyone can understand how to set up and manage an online store successfully.

1. Product Catalog

- **Definition**: A product catalog is a digital inventory where all the items you sell are listed with details like names, descriptions, prices, and images.
- **Importance**: A well-organized product catalog helps customers easily find and understand what you're selling. It also plays a crucial role in attracting potential buyers and encouraging them to make a purchase.
- **Key Features**:
  - **Product Descriptions**: Clear and concise descriptions that explain the product's features, benefits, and specifications.
  - **High-Quality Images**: Multiple images showing the product from different angles.
  - **Search and Filters**: Tools that allow customers to search for specific products or filter items based on categories, prices, sizes, colors, etc.

2. Shopping Cart

- **Definition**: A shopping cart is a feature that allows customers to select and store products they want to buy while they continue browsing your store.
- **Importance**: The shopping cart is a crucial part of the e-commerce experience because it helps customers keep track of the items they intend to purchase. It also simplifies the checkout process by gathering all selected items in one place.
- **Key Features**:
  - **Add to Cart**: A button on each product page that allows customers to add items to their cart.
  - **Cart Summary**: A section where customers can view the total cost, including taxes and shipping fees.
  - **Save for Later**: An option for customers to save items in their cart for a future purchase.

3. Checkout Process

- **Definition**: The checkout process is the series of steps customers go through to complete their purchase, from reviewing their cart to making payment.
- **Importance**: A smooth and straightforward checkout process reduces cart abandonment and increases the likelihood of completing sales. The easier it is for customers to check out, the better their shopping experience will be.
- **Key Features**:
  - **Guest Checkout**: Allows customers to make a purchase without creating an account, making the process quicker.
  - **Multiple Payment Options**: Offers various payment methods, such as credit/debit cards, PayPal, and other digital wallets.
  - **Shipping Options**: Provides different shipping methods and allows customers to choose their preferred option.
  - **Order Confirmation**: Sends an email to the customer confirming the details of their purchase.

4. Payment Gateway Integration

- **Definition**: A payment gateway is a service that processes payments made through your website, ensuring that transactions are secure.
- **Importance**: Without a reliable payment gateway, customers cannot pay for the products or services they want to buy. It's essential for handling payments securely and protecting both the customer and the business from fraud.
- **Key Features**:
  - **Secure Transactions**: Encryption technology to protect sensitive customer data.
  - **Support for Multiple Currencies**: Allows customers to pay in their preferred currency.
  - **Fraud Detection**: Tools to identify and prevent fraudulent transactions.

5. Inventory Management

- **Definition**: Inventory management is the system that tracks and manages the products you have in stock, ensuring that your store always has the right amount of products available.
- **Importance**: Good inventory management helps prevent issues like overselling (selling products you don't have in stock) and stockouts (running out of products), both of which can lead to dissatisfied customers.
- **Key Features**:
  - **Stock Levels**: Automatically updates the quantity of each product as sales are made.
  - **Low Stock Alerts**: Notifies you when a product is running low, so you can reorder before running out.
  - **Automated Reordering**: Automatically places orders with suppliers when stock reaches a certain level.

6. Customer Accounts and Profiles

- **Definition**: Customer accounts allow users to create a profile on your website, where they can manage their orders, track shipments, and save their details for future purchases.

- **Importance**: While guest checkout is essential, offering customer accounts can enhance the shopping experience by making repeat purchases easier and allowing customers to manage their preferences.
  - **Key Features**:
    - **Order History**: Allows customers to view their past purchases.
    - **Wish Lists**: Lets customers save products they're interested in buying later.
    - **Saved Payment Information**: Allows customers to save their payment details for faster checkout next time.

7. Shipping and Delivery Options

  - **Definition**: Shipping and delivery options are the methods by which products are delivered to customers after they make a purchase.
  - **Importance**: Offering flexible and reliable shipping options is crucial for meeting customer expectations and ensuring they receive their orders on time.
  - **Key Features**:
    - **Multiple Shipping Methods**: Standard, expedited, and international shipping options.
    - **Shipping Calculators**: Shows customers the cost of shipping based on their location.
    - **Tracking Information**: Provides customers with a tracking number to follow their package's journey.

8. Customer Support and Service

  - **Definition**: Customer support refers to the assistance you provide to customers before, during, and after their purchase.
  - **Importance**: Good customer support can enhance customer satisfaction and loyalty. It's also essential for resolving any issues that may arise, such as questions about products or problems with orders.
  - **Key Features**:
    - **Live Chat**: Offers real-time assistance to customers as they browse your site.
    - **FAQs**: A section with answers to common questions to help customers quickly find the information they need.

- **Returns and Refunds**: A clear and simple process for handling product returns and refunds.

Conclusion

E-commerce functionality is the backbone of a successful online store. By ensuring that your website includes essential features like a well-organized product catalog, a user-friendly shopping cart, a smooth checkout process, secure payment gateway integration, and effective inventory management, you can create a seamless shopping experience for your customers. Additionally, offering customer accounts, flexible shipping options, and reliable customer support will help build trust and encourage repeat business. Whether you're just starting or looking to improve your existing online store, focusing on these key areas will help you meet the needs of your customers and achieve your business goals.

8.Testing and Launch

Steps for Website Testing

Website testing is a crucial process to ensure that your site works properly, looks good, and provides a great user experience. Testing helps identify and fix issues before your website goes live, preventing problems that could affect visitors' experience or cause your site to malfunction. Here's a simple guide to the essential steps for effective website testing:

1. Plan Your Testing

- **Definition**: Planning involves determining what aspects of your website need to be tested and how you will conduct the tests.

- **Importance**: Proper planning ensures that you cover all necessary areas and test thoroughly, avoiding overlooked issues.
  - **Steps**:
    - **Identify Testing Goals**: Decide what you need to test, such as functionality, usability, performance, and security.
    - **Create a Testing Checklist**: List all the elements and features of your site that need to be tested.

2. Functional Testing

- **Definition**: Functional testing checks whether your website's features and functions work as intended.
- **Importance**: Ensures that all parts of your site operate correctly and that users can interact with it as expected.
- **Steps**:
  - **Test Navigation**: Verify that all menus, links, and buttons direct users to the correct pages.
  - **Check Forms**: Ensure that all forms (contact forms, registration forms) submit data correctly and show appropriate messages for errors or successful submissions.
  - **Verify Transactions**: If you have an e-commerce site, test the shopping cart, checkout process, and payment gateway.

3. Usability Testing

- **Definition**: Usability testing evaluates how user-friendly and intuitive your website is.
- **Importance**: Helps improve the overall user experience by ensuring that visitors can easily navigate and use your site.
- **Steps**:
  - **Conduct User Surveys**: Gather feedback from real users to understand their experience and identify areas for improvement.
  - **Observe User Behavior**: Watch how users interact with your site to spot any difficulties or confusion.
  - **Check Mobile Compatibility**: Ensure your site is easy to use on different devices, such as smartphones and tablets.

4. Performance Testing

- **Definition**: Performance testing measures how well your website performs under various conditions, such as different levels of traffic.
- **Importance**: Ensures that your site loads quickly and remains stable even during high traffic periods.
- **Steps**:
  - **Test Load Time**: Use tools to measure how fast your site's pages load and optimize them if needed.
  - **Check Stress Handling**: Simulate high traffic to see how your site performs under heavy load.
  - **Monitor Server Response**: Ensure that your server responds quickly to requests.

5. Compatibility Testing

- **Definition**: Compatibility testing ensures that your website works correctly across different browsers, devices, and operating systems.
- **Importance**: Guarantees that all users, regardless of their device or browser, have a consistent experience.
- **Steps**:
  - **Test on Multiple Browsers**: Verify that your site functions well on popular browsers like Chrome, Firefox, Safari, and Edge.
  - **Check Different Devices**: Test your site on various devices, including desktops, tablets, and smartphones.
  - **Ensure Cross-Platform Compatibility**: Confirm that your site works across different operating systems, such as Windows, macOS, iOS, and Android.

6. Security Testing

- **Definition**: Security testing identifies vulnerabilities and ensures that your website is protected from potential threats.
- **Importance**: Protects your site from cyberattacks, data breaches, and other security risks.
- **Steps**:
  - **Check for Vulnerabilities**: Use security tools to scan for potential vulnerabilities in your site's code and infrastructure.

- **Verify HTTPS**: Ensure that your site uses HTTPS to encrypt data transmitted between the user and your server.
  - **Test for Data Protection**: Confirm that sensitive information, such as user data and payment details, is securely stored and handled.

7. Regression Testing

- **Definition**: Regression testing involves rechecking your site after changes or updates to ensure that new changes haven't introduced new issues.
- **Importance**: Ensures that updates or fixes do not negatively impact existing features or functionality.
- **Steps**:
  - **Re-run Previous Tests**: Perform previously conducted tests to ensure that everything still works correctly after changes.
  - **Verify New Features**: Check that any new features or updates function as expected and do not affect other parts of the site.

8. User Acceptance Testing (UAT)

- **Definition**: UAT involves testing the website with real users to ensure it meets their needs and expectations.
- **Importance**: Provides final validation from the perspective of actual users, confirming that the site is ready for launch.
- **Steps**:
  - **Select Test Users**: Choose a group of real users to test the site.
  - **Conduct Testing Sessions**: Have users perform typical tasks on the site and gather feedback.
  - **Review Feedback**: Address any issues or concerns raised by users before finalizing the site.

Conclusion

Website testing is a multi-step process that helps ensure your site is functional, user-friendly, and secure. By planning your testing, checking functionality, usability, performance, compatibility, security, and performing regression and user acceptance testing, you can identify and fix issues before your site goes live. Thorough testing not only enhances the quality of your website but also provides a better experience for your users, leading to greater satisfaction and success.

Pre-Launch Checklist for Your Website

Before launching your website, it's crucial to ensure that everything is ready to provide a smooth experience for your visitors and avoid potential issues. A pre-launch checklist helps you systematically review all aspects of your site, making sure it functions correctly and meets your goals. Here's a simple guide to a comprehensive pre-launch checklist to help you prepare for a successful website launch.

1. Review Website Content

- **Definition**: Content review involves checking all text, images, videos, and other media on your site.
- **Importance**: Ensures that your content is accurate, relevant, and free of errors, which helps create a professional and trustworthy image.
- **Steps**:
  - **Proofread Text**: Check for spelling and grammatical errors in all written content.
  - **Verify Media**: Ensure that all images and videos load correctly and are displayed at the right size and quality.
  - **Check Links**: Test all internal and external links to make sure they direct users to the correct pages.

2. Test Website Functionality

- **Definition**: Functionality testing checks whether all interactive elements on your website work as intended.
- **Importance**: Guarantees that users can navigate your site, complete forms, and use features without issues.
- **Steps**:
  - **Test Forms**: Ensure all forms (contact, registration, etc.) submit data correctly and provide confirmation messages.

- **Verify Buttons and Links**: Check that all buttons and links direct users to the correct pages or perform the desired actions.
  - **Check E-Commerce Features**: For online stores, test the shopping cart, checkout process, and payment gateway.

3. Verify Mobile and Browser Compatibility

- **Definition**: Compatibility testing ensures that your website looks and functions properly across different devices and web browsers.
- **Importance**: Ensures a consistent experience for all users, regardless of their device or browser choice.
- **Steps**:
  - **Test on Multiple Devices**: Check how your site appears and functions on desktops, tablets, and smartphones.
  - **Check Different Browsers**: Test your site on popular browsers such as Chrome, Firefox, Safari, and Edge.
  - **Adjust for Screen Sizes**: Make sure your site adjusts to various screen sizes and resolutions.

4. Ensure Website Security

- **Definition**: Security testing identifies and addresses vulnerabilities to protect your site from potential threats.
- **Importance**: Safeguards user data and maintains the integrity of your site.
- **Steps**:
  - **Install SSL Certificate**: Ensure your site uses HTTPS to encrypt data transmitted between users and your server.
  - **Check for Vulnerabilities**: Use security tools to scan for potential security issues and fix any identified vulnerabilities.
  - **Update Software**: Ensure that all software, plugins, and themes are up-to-date with the latest security patches.

5. Optimize Website Performance

- **Definition**: Performance optimization involves improving the speed and responsiveness of your site.

- **Importance**: A fast-loading site provides a better user experience and can improve search engine rankings.
- **Steps**:
  - **Check Load Times**: Use tools to measure how quickly your pages load and optimize them if necessary.
  - **Optimize Images**: Compress and resize images to reduce their impact on loading times.
  - **Enable Caching**: Set up caching to speed up the delivery of your site's content to users.

6. Set Up Analytics and Tracking

- **Definition**: Analytics and tracking involve setting up tools to monitor and analyze your website's performance and user behavior.
- **Importance**: Provides insights into how users interact with your site and helps you make data-driven decisions.
- **Steps**:
  - **Install Google Analytics**: Add Google Analytics or another tracking tool to monitor visitor behavior, traffic sources, and more.
  - **Set Up Conversion Tracking**: Track key actions on your site, such as form submissions or product purchases.
  - **Review Metrics**: Familiarize yourself with the metrics you'll be monitoring to understand user engagement and site performance.

7. Check SEO Elements

- **Definition**: SEO (Search Engine Optimization) elements are aspects of your site that affect how it ranks in search engine results.
- **Importance**: Helps improve your site's visibility and ranking in search engines, attracting more visitors.
- **Steps**:
  - **Review Meta Tags**: Ensure each page has a unique and descriptive meta title and meta description.
  - **Check Keywords**: Verify that your content includes relevant keywords naturally.
  - **Optimize URL Structure**: Use clean, descriptive URLs for your pages.

8. Finalize Legal and Compliance Aspects

- **Definition**: Legal and compliance checks ensure your site adheres to relevant laws and regulations.
- **Importance**: Protects you from legal issues and ensures that your site meets regulatory requirements.
- **Steps**:
  - **Add Privacy Policy**: Include a privacy policy detailing how you collect, use, and protect user data.
  - **Include Terms and Conditions**: Provide terms and conditions outlining the rules for using your site.
  - **Ensure Accessibility**: Make sure your site is accessible to users with disabilities by following accessibility guidelines.

9. Conduct a Pre-Launch Review

- **Definition**: A final review involves thoroughly examining all aspects of your site before it goes live.
- **Importance**: Helps catch any last-minute issues and ensures everything is in order for launch.
- **Steps**:
  - **Review All Content**: Double-check all text, images, and media for accuracy and completeness.
  - **Test All Features**: Ensure that every feature, form, and function works correctly.
  - **Get Feedback**: Ask a few people to use your site and provide feedback on their experience.

Conclusion

A pre-launch checklist is essential for ensuring that your website is ready for visitors and functions smoothly. By reviewing content, testing functionality, ensuring compatibility, securing your site, optimizing performance, setting up analytics, checking SEO elements, and addressing legal aspects, you can avoid common issues and provide a positive experience for your users. A thorough pre-launch review helps identify and fix any problems before your site goes live, contributing to a successful and seamless launch.

9. Maintenance and Updates

Regular Updates and Security Measures

Maintaining a website is not a one-time task; it requires ongoing attention to ensure it remains secure, up-to-date, and functioning properly. Regular updates and implementing strong security measures are crucial to protecting your website from potential threats and keeping it running smoothly. Here's a straightforward explanation of why these aspects are important and how you can manage them effectively.

1. Importance of Regular Updates

- **Definition**: Regular updates involve routinely updating your website's software, plugins, themes, and content.
- **Importance**: Keeping your website up-to-date ensures that it continues to work correctly and efficiently while reducing the risk of security vulnerabilities.
- **Steps**:
  - **Update Software**: Websites are often built using content management systems (CMS) like WordPress, Joomla, or Drupal. These platforms regularly release updates that fix bugs, improve performance, and patch security flaws. Regularly updating your CMS is crucial to ensure it functions properly and stays secure.
  - **Update Plugins and Themes**: Plugins and themes add functionality and design to your website. However, outdated plugins or themes can become incompatible with your CMS or have security gaps that hackers can exploit. Regularly check for updates and apply them to keep your site running smoothly.

- **Content Updates**: Regularly updating your content is also important. Fresh content keeps your site relevant and engaging to visitors, which can improve your search engine rankings. Additionally, updating old content with new information ensures that it remains accurate and useful.

2. Importance of Security Measures

- **Definition**: Security measures are practices and tools used to protect your website from threats like hacking, malware, and data breaches.
- **Importance**: Strong security measures help prevent unauthorized access to your site, protect sensitive data, and ensure your website remains available and trustworthy to users.
- **Steps**:
  - **Install Security Plugins**: Security plugins help protect your site by scanning for vulnerabilities, blocking malicious traffic, and offering additional security features like firewalls and login protection. For example, if you're using WordPress, plugins like Wordfence or Sucuri can enhance your site's security.
  - **Use Strong Passwords**: Weak passwords are one of the most common ways hackers gain access to websites. Use strong, complex passwords for all user accounts, especially admin accounts. Consider using a password manager to generate and store secure passwords.
  - **Enable Two-Factor Authentication (2FA)**: Two-factor authentication adds an extra layer of security by requiring a second form of verification (like a code sent to your phone) in addition to your password. This makes it much harder for hackers to gain access to your site, even if they have your password.
  - **Secure Your Hosting Environment**: Choose a reliable hosting provider that offers robust security features, such as regular backups, SSL certificates, and protection against Distributed Denial of Service (DDoS) attacks. Secure hosting environments reduce the risk of your website being compromised.
  - **Regular Backups**: Regularly backing up your website ensures that you have a copy of your site's data in case of a security breach or data loss. Many hosting providers offer automatic backups, but you should

also consider setting up additional backup solutions that store copies in different locations, such as on the cloud.

3. Monitoring and Managing Website Security

- **Definition**: Monitoring involves keeping an eye on your website's activity to detect any unusual or suspicious behavior. Managing security means actively taking steps to prevent and respond to threats.
- **Importance**: Proactive monitoring and management help you catch potential security issues early and minimize the impact of any attacks on your site.
- **Steps**:
  - **Monitor Traffic and Logs**: Use tools to monitor your website's traffic and server logs for any unusual activity, such as sudden spikes in traffic, multiple failed login attempts, or changes to files. Tools like Google Analytics and security plugins can help you monitor your site effectively.
  - **Scan for Malware**: Regularly scan your site for malware or other malicious code that could compromise your site's security. Many security plugins offer malware scanning features, or you can use online tools for a more thorough check.
  - **Respond to Threats Promptly**: If you detect a security issue, take immediate action to address it. This may involve restoring your site from a backup, changing passwords, or working with your hosting provider to resolve the issue.

4. Educating Your Team

- **Definition**: Educating your team means ensuring that everyone who has access to your website knows how to follow security best practices.
- **Importance**: Even the most secure website can be vulnerable if team members don't follow good security practices. Educating your team helps prevent accidental security breaches.
- **Steps**:
  - **Train on Security Practices**: Provide training on how to create strong passwords, recognize phishing attempts, and avoid risky online behaviors. Regularly update training to include new threats and best practices.

- **Limit Access**: Only give access to your website's backend to those who need it. The fewer people with access, the lower the risk of a security breach. Use role-based access controls to restrict access to sensitive areas of your site.

Conclusion

Regular updates and robust security measures are essential to keeping your website secure and running smoothly. By regularly updating your software, plugins, and content, and implementing strong security practices like using security plugins, strong passwords, and monitoring for threats, you can protect your site from potential risks. Additionally, educating your team and limiting access helps further safeguard your website. By staying proactive and vigilant, you can ensure that your website remains a safe and reliable resource for your visitors.

Performance Monitoring

Performance monitoring is the process of continuously tracking and analyzing your website's performance to ensure it runs smoothly, loads quickly, and provides a positive experience for users. By regularly monitoring your website's performance, you can identify and address issues before they impact your visitors, helping to maintain your site's reliability and effectiveness.

Here's an easy-to-understand explanation of why performance monitoring is important and how you can implement it.

1. Why Performance Monitoring is Important

- **User Experience**: A fast and reliable website provides a better experience for users. If your website is slow or frequently goes down, visitors are likely to leave and may not return. Performance monitoring helps you identify issues that could negatively affect user experience, such as slow loading times or broken features, so you can fix them quickly.

- **Search Engine Rankings**: Search engines like Google consider website performance when determining search rankings. A well-performing site is more likely to rank higher in search results, which can lead to more traffic. Performance monitoring helps you ensure your site meets the standards set by search engines.

- **Business Impact**: For businesses, website performance directly impacts revenue. Slow load times or downtime can lead to lost sales, lower conversion rates, and a negative brand reputation. Regular monitoring ensures your site is always running at its best, minimizing potential losses.

2. Key Aspects of Performance Monitoring

- **Page Load Speed**: This is the time it takes for a web page to fully load and become interactive. Faster page load speeds lead to a better user experience and higher search engine rankings. You can monitor page load speed using tools like Google PageSpeed Insights or GTmetrix. These tools analyze your website and provide suggestions for improving load times.

- **Uptime Monitoring**: Uptime refers to the amount of time your website is online and accessible to users. Downtime, on the other hand, is when your site is unavailable. Uptime monitoring tools, such as UptimeRobot or Pingdom, constantly check your site to ensure it's online and notify you if it goes down. Maintaining high uptime is crucial for providing a reliable service to your users.

- **Server Performance**: Your website's performance is heavily influenced by the server it's hosted on. Monitoring server performance involves tracking factors like CPU usage, memory usage, and disk space. If your server is overloaded or experiencing issues, it can slow down your site or cause it to crash. Many hosting providers offer built-in monitoring tools, or you can use third-party services like New Relic or Datadog.

- **Mobile Performance**: With more people accessing websites on their mobile devices, it's essential to monitor how your site performs on smartphones and tablets. Mobile performance monitoring ensures that your site loads quickly and functions well on smaller screens. Google's Mobile-Friendly Test is a useful tool for checking how your site performs on mobile devices.

- **Content Delivery Network (CDN) Performance**: A CDN is a network of servers distributed across different locations that deliver content to users based on their geographic location. Using a CDN can significantly speed up your website, especially for international visitors. Monitoring your CDN's performance ensures it's delivering content efficiently and that there are no bottlenecks.

3. Tools and Techniques for Performance Monitoring

- **Google Analytics**: Google Analytics is a free tool that provides detailed insights into your website's performance, including load times, traffic sources, and user behavior. You can use it to track page speed, identify slow pages, and see how performance issues affect user engagement.

- **GTmetrix**: GTmetrix analyzes your website's speed and provides a detailed report on what's slowing it down. It also offers recommendations for improving performance, such as optimizing images or minifying code.

- **Pingdom**: Pingdom monitors your website's uptime and speed, alerting you if there are any issues. It also provides historical data so you can track performance trends over time.

- **New Relic**: New Relic is a comprehensive monitoring tool that tracks server performance, application performance, and user experience. It's particularly useful for complex websites with heavy traffic or custom applications.

- **Regular Audits**: In addition to using monitoring tools, conducting regular performance audits is a good practice. Audits involve a thorough review of your site's performance, identifying areas for improvement, and implementing changes to enhance speed and reliability.

4. Responding to Performance Issues

- **Identify the Problem**: When performance monitoring tools alert you to an issue, the first step is to identify the problem. Is the site slow due to high traffic, a server issue, or a coding error? Understanding the cause is crucial for resolving the issue effectively.

- **Implement Solutions**: Once you've identified the problem, take action to fix it. This might involve optimizing images, upgrading your hosting plan, or fixing broken code. Many performance monitoring tools provide specific recommendations to help you address issues.

- **Test and Re-Monitor**: After implementing solutions, test your website again to ensure the issue has been resolved. Continue monitoring your site's performance to catch any new problems that may arise.

Conclusion

Performance monitoring is essential for maintaining a fast, reliable, and user-friendly website. By regularly tracking key aspects like page load speed, uptime, server performance, and mobile performance, you can identify and fix issues before they impact your users. Using tools like Google Analytics, GTmetrix, and Pingdom makes performance monitoring more manageable, ensuring that your website remains a valuable resource for your visitors and a strong asset for your business.

10.Conclusion

Measuring Website Success

Once your website is up and running, it's important to measure its success to understand whether it's achieving your goals and delivering value to your visitors. Measuring website success involves analyzing various metrics and key performance indicators (KPIs) to determine how well your site is performing and where improvements may be needed. Here's a simple guide to help you understand how to measure the success of your website.

1. Setting Clear Goals

Before you can measure success, you need to define what success looks like for your website. This involves setting clear, measurable goals that align with your overall business objectives. Common goals might include increasing traffic, generating leads, improving user engagement, or driving sales. By setting specific goals, you can focus your measurement efforts on the metrics that matter most to you.

- **Example Goals**:
  - Increase website traffic by 20% over the next six months.
  - Achieve a 10% conversion rate on product pages.
  - Reduce bounce rate by 15% within three months.

2. Key Performance Indicators (KPIs)

KPIs are specific metrics that help you track progress toward your goals. Different websites will have different KPIs depending on their purpose. For instance, an e-commerce site might focus on sales and conversion rates, while a blog might prioritize traffic and engagement. Below are some common KPIs to consider:

- **Traffic Metrics**:
  - **Page Views**: The number of times a page is viewed. High page views indicate that your content is attracting visitors.

- **Unique Visitors**: The number of distinct individuals visiting your site. Tracking unique visitors helps you understand the reach of your website.
  - **Traffic Sources**: Identifying where your visitors are coming from—search engines, social media, direct visits, or referrals—can help you focus your marketing efforts.

- **Engagement Metrics**:
  - **Bounce Rate**: The percentage of visitors who leave your site after viewing only one page. A high bounce rate may indicate that your content isn't engaging or relevant to visitors.
  - **Average Session Duration**: The average amount of time visitors spend on your site. Longer sessions generally indicate more engaging content.
  - **Pages Per Session**: The average number of pages viewed during a visit. More pages per session often suggest that visitors find your site valuable and are exploring more content.

- **Conversion Metrics**:
  - **Conversion Rate**: The percentage of visitors who complete a desired action, such as making a purchase, signing up for a newsletter, or filling out a contact form. A high conversion rate indicates that your website is effective at driving desired actions.
  - **Cart Abandonment Rate**: For e-commerce sites, this measures how often visitors add items to their cart but don't complete the purchase. Reducing cart abandonment can lead to more sales.

- **SEO Metrics**:
  - **Search Engine Rankings**: Monitoring where your site ranks for important keywords in search engine results can give you insights into your SEO performance.
  - **Organic Traffic**: The number of visitors coming to your site through search engines. High organic traffic usually means your SEO efforts are paying off.

3. Tools for Measuring Website Success

There are several tools available that can help you measure your website's performance and track your KPIs:

- **Google Analytics**: This is a powerful, free tool that provides detailed insights into your website's traffic, user behavior, and conversions. Google Analytics allows you to track metrics like page views, bounce rate, and conversion rate, and it offers customizable reports to monitor your progress toward your goals.

- **Google Search Console**: This tool helps you monitor your website's presence in Google search results. It provides data on search queries that bring visitors to your site, your average position in search results, and any issues that might affect your search visibility.

- **Heatmaps (e.g., Hotjar)**: Heatmaps show you where users click, scroll, and spend the most time on your website. This information can help you understand user behavior and optimize your site's layout and content.

- **A/B Testing Tools**: Tools like Optimizely or Google Optimize allow you to run experiments on your website to see which versions of a page perform better. This can help you optimize conversions by testing different headlines, images, or call-to-action buttons.

4. Analyzing and Interpreting Data

Collecting data is only the first step. The next step is to analyze and interpret that data to make informed decisions about your website. Here's how you can approach this:

- **Compare Against Goals**: Regularly compare your performance metrics against the goals you set. Are you meeting your targets? If not, what might be causing the shortfall?

- **Identify Trends**: Look for trends in your data over time. For example, if your bounce rate is gradually increasing, it could indicate that your content needs improvement or that there's a technical issue affecting user experience.

- **Understand User Behavior**: Use tools like Google Analytics and heatmaps to understand how users interact with your site. Are they engaging with your content? Are they following the desired user journey? Understanding user behavior can help you make changes to improve engagement and conversions.

5. Continuous Improvement

Measuring website success is not a one-time task—it's an ongoing process. Regularly review your KPIs, analyze your data, and make adjustments to your website to keep improving its performance. This could involve updating content, optimizing for SEO, improving site speed, or refining your marketing strategies.

Conclusion

Measuring website success is crucial to understanding how well your site is performing and ensuring it meets your goals. By setting clear goals, tracking relevant KPIs, using the right tools, and continuously analyzing your data, you can gain valuable insights into your website's strengths and areas for improvement. This ongoing process of measurement and optimization will help you create a more effective and successful website that delivers value to both your business and your visitors.

Future Planning

Future planning is the process of setting goals and outlining strategies to achieve them in the coming years. It involves thinking ahead, anticipating potential challenges, and preparing for changes that may impact your personal life or business. By carefully planning for the future, you can position yourself or your business to take advantage of opportunities and navigate difficulties more effectively.

Here's a simple guide to understanding the importance of future planning and how to approach it.

1. Importance of Future Planning

- **Direction and Focus**: Future planning gives you a clear sense of direction. It helps you understand where you want to go and how you can get there. Without a plan, it's easy to get distracted or make decisions that don't align with your long-term goals. Planning for the future ensures that your efforts are focused on achieving the outcomes you desire.

- **Risk Management**: Planning for the future allows you to anticipate potential risks and challenges. By identifying these in advance, you can develop strategies to mitigate them. For example, a business might plan for economic downturns by building a financial cushion or diversifying its income streams. Similarly, in personal life, planning for retirement ensures financial stability in later years.

- **Adaptability**: The world is constantly changing, and future planning helps you stay adaptable. By thinking ahead, you can prepare for changes in technology, market conditions, or personal circumstances. This adaptability is crucial for long-term success, as it allows you to pivot and adjust your strategies when necessary.

- **Resource Management**: Effective future planning helps you allocate resources more efficiently. Whether it's time, money, or human resources, planning ensures that these are used in the most productive way. For instance, a company might plan its budget to ensure sufficient funds for research and development, while an individual might plan their savings to ensure they can afford a home or education.

2. Steps to Effective Future Planning

- **Set Clear Goals**: The first step in future planning is to set clear, specific goals. These should be realistic and achievable, but also challenging enough to inspire progress. For example, a business goal might be to expand into new markets within the next five years, while a personal goal might be to achieve financial independence by a certain age.

- **Conduct a SWOT Analysis**: SWOT stands for Strengths, Weaknesses, Opportunities, and Threats. Conducting a SWOT analysis helps you understand where you currently stand and what factors could impact your future. By identifying your strengths, you can leverage them to achieve your goals. Recognizing your weaknesses allows you to address them, while understanding opportunities and threats helps you plan for external factors.

- **Create a Strategic Plan**: Once you have your goals and a clear understanding of your current situation, the next step is to create a strategic plan. This plan should outline the steps you need to take to achieve your goals, along with timelines and milestones. For example, if your goal is to start a new business, your strategic plan might include steps like conducting market research, securing funding, and launching a marketing campaign.

- **Prepare for Contingencies**: It's important to plan for unexpected events that could derail your progress. This could involve creating a contingency plan that outlines how you will respond to various scenarios, such as a sudden drop in sales or an unexpected expense. Having a backup plan in place ensures that you're not caught off guard and can continue moving forward even when things don't go as planned.

- **Regularly Review and Adjust**: Future planning is not a one-time task; it requires regular review and adjustment. As time goes on, your goals and circumstances may change, and your plan should evolve accordingly. Regularly reviewing your progress and making necessary adjustments ensures that you stay on track and continue to move toward your long-term objectives.

3. Long-Term vs. Short-Term Planning

When planning for the future, it's important to consider both long-term and short-term goals.

- **Long-Term Planning**: This involves setting goals that you aim to achieve over several years or even decades. Long-term planning requires you to think about where you want to be in the distant future and what major steps you need to take to get there. For example, long-term business planning might involve expanding internationally or developing a new product line. In personal life, it could mean planning for retirement or buying a home.

- **Short-Term Planning**: Short-term planning focuses on goals that you can achieve within a year or less. These are often the smaller steps that contribute to your long-term goals. For instance, a short-term goal might be to complete a professional certification or launch a new marketing campaign. Short-term planning helps you make steady progress and maintain momentum.

4. Tools for Future Planning

There are various tools and methods that can assist in future planning:

- **Gantt Charts**: Gantt charts are visual tools that help you plan and schedule tasks over time. They are especially useful for project management, allowing you to see at a glance how different tasks overlap and what needs to be done by when.

- **Financial Planning Tools**: For personal or business financial planning, tools like budgeting apps, retirement calculators, and investment trackers can help you manage your finances and plan for the future.

- **Mind Mapping**: Mind maps are a creative way to brainstorm and organize ideas. They can be particularly helpful in the early stages of planning, allowing you to explore different possibilities and see how various aspects of your plan connect.

Conclusion

Future planning is essential for anyone who wants to achieve their long-term goals and navigate life's uncertainties with confidence. By setting clear goals, creating a strategic plan, and regularly reviewing your progress, you can stay on track and make informed decisions that will lead to success. Whether for personal life or business, effective future planning ensures that you are prepared for whatever comes your way, allowing you to take advantage of opportunities and overcome challenges as they arise.

Closing Note:

As you reach the end of **"Mastering Website Creation: A Step-by-Step Guide to Building Successful Websites,"** we hope you feel empowered and inspired to embark on your own website creation journey. This book has been designed to equip you with the knowledge and tools necessary to transform your vision into a compelling, functional online presence.

Building a website is more than just a technical endeavor; it's about creating a space that reflects your passion, showcases your unique ideas, and connects with your audience. Remember, every great website starts with a single step, and with the guidance provided in this book, you are well-prepared to take that step confidently.

We encourage you to revisit the concepts, apply the techniques, and continue refining your skills. The digital world is constantly evolving, and so can your website. Keep learning, stay curious, and always strive for excellence.

Thank you for choosing **"Mastering Website Creation."** We wish you great success in your website endeavors and hope your online journey is as fulfilling as it is rewarding. Your next masterpiece is just a few clicks away!

www.ingramcontent.com/pod-product-compliance
Lightning Source LLC
Chambersburg PA
CBHW030504220526
45464CB00006B/2651